LOOKING BACK AT
TIMPERLEY

Hazel Pryor

Willow
PUBLISHING

© Willow Publishing 1982

Willow Publishing
Willow Cottage, 36 Moss Lane,
Timperley, Altrincham,
Cheshire, WA15 6SZ

ISBN 0 9506043 8 0

Printed by The Commercial
Centre Ltd., Clowes Street,
Hollinwood, Oldham.

Below: Thorley Lane. This thatched cottage was for many years the home of John Lanceley, who had the added problem of stray footballs from the yard of the Mixed School next door. Thorley Lane has changed so much that the only building recognisable now is the Church in the distance. Lanceley's Cottage has disappeared apart from the large pear tree on the corner of Mainwood Road, which stood in the garden, and the School was replaced by Christ Church Hall, even the stone wall being moved back to allow for road widening.

During the time I worked at Altrincham Library, the lack of a book about Timperley was obvious with the enquiries received from people interested in the history of the area, whether they were children doing school projects or older people reviving memories or even settling arguments. The local history books about Altrincham hardly mention Timperley, the records are available but are cumbersome to use, and many of the older residents have died or moved from the area.

This book will not answer all the questions, but I hope it will provide a few answers, perhaps revive memories for some people and give an outline history of Timperley for youngsters or newcomers.

I would like to thank the staff at Altrincham Library for their patience and assistance over the years, and all the people who have provided information and memories. Regretfully I have not been able to include all the photographs which have been lent, but I would sincerely like to thank *everyone* who has gone to the trouble of searching out old postcards and family photographs. Thanks must go also to all the people who have treasured (or hoarded) items over the years, and perhaps most of all to the photographers themselves, who recorded for us the Timperley of 80 years ago.

I would like to thank the following for permission to reproduce photographs:
Mrs. H. Anson, Mr. B. Arnold, Mr. A. Baguley, Mr. B. Bradbury, Mr. D. Cleary, Mrs. E. Davenport, Mr. J. Dean, Mrs. E. Eglin, Mr. L. Garner, Mr. K. Greenwood, Mr. K. Healey, Mrs. Hedgecox, Mrs. E. Jackson, Mr. R. F. Jackson, Mrs. Maddocks, Mrs. J. Minifie, Mrs. Patchett, Mrs. Rodney, Mr. L. Ryan, Mr. G. Sant, Mrs. J. Stone, Mrs. Sumner, Mr. J. Whiteley, and the Borough Librarian of Trafford.

For those who wish to delve deeper (and I hope at least a few people will), I have listed a few useful items, some available in the bookshops, others at Altrincham Library.

Balshaw's Stranger's guide and complete directory to Altrincham, etc. 1859 (reprinted 1973).
Bygone Altrincham: traditions and history, by Charles Nickson. 1935 (reprinted 1971).
A History of Altrincham and Bowdon, by Alfred Ingham. 1879.
Slater's Directory of Altrincham, Bowdon, Sale, etc. Annual series covering about 1900 to 1916.
(For Baguley)
Wythenshawe: a history of the townships of Northenden, Northern Etchells, and Baguley. Vol.1: to 1926. Edited by W. H. Shercliff. 1974.

Hazel Pryor
Timperley 1982

Introduction

Many people now living in Timperley can hardly imagine it as anything but a suburban area, with most of the houses dating from the 1930s or later and only a few older ones. So this book will look at what the area was like before the housing developments of the 1930s, with just a few glances at the 1940s and 1950s.

Up to the early 19th century Timperley was one of several 'townships' in the large Parish of Bowdon, and the affairs of the township were run by the local farmers who took it in turn to be the officers responsible for the care of the poor, the upkeep of the roads and keeping the peace. Gradually during the 19th century these affairs were taken over by various county and district boards, and by 1900 most aspects were being dealt with by Bucklow Rural District Council, leaving Timperley Parish Council with very little to do.

Altrincham, meanwhile, had been growing and developing, but by 1910 had become very short of land for house building. Timperley still had acres of open farm land, so Altrincham Urban District Council proposed amalgamation. However it took another 20 years before this was finally achieved in 1936, and then Timperley started to change.

In the early 13th century a man called Walter of Timperley (spelled Timperleie) was a witness to a charter. The charter itself does not concern us, but this was one of the earliest references to the name Timperley. The most commonly accepted explanation of the name comes from the words 'timber', and 'leah' meaning a clearing or glade. The ending -ley is a common one locally, we have only to think of Baguley (badger-ley), Ashley, Mobberley and others. The name has gone through various forms, spelled phonetically, with a 'y' at the beginning and variations of 'legh' at the end, but the present spelling is remarkably close to the early form.

An alternative explanation known locally is that the name arises from the name 'tymp' given to stone blocks, or troughs, quarried locally. For this to be feasible, the quarries would have had to be well-established by the 13th century at the latest, and no documentary reference has yet been found earlier than the 17th century.

The early settlement in Timperley, possibly in Saxon times, was probably on the higher ground near the junction of Wood Lane and Green Lane, with open fields extending to the north and east keeping to the higher land. The cultivated land was gradually extended, while separate moated farmsteads were set up nearer to the Timperley and Fairywell Brooks which form the boundary of Timperley. Timperley Hall and Riddings Hall were two of these farmsteads and there was probably another moat at the Heyes, off Heyes Lane, but no information has been found about this.

Most of the centre of Timperley consisted of Timperley Moss and common land. The Common included the area of the Village and probably extended northwards until it joined up with the Moss. The Moss covered most of the land between Park Road and Deansgate Lane, extending beyond the Canal and to about half way down Grove Lane.

In 1475 the Moss and Common were divided among the three main landowners – John Arderne of Timperley Hall, Sir William Booth and William Buckley (or Bulkeley). It was important as a source of peat for fuel, and in 1584 William Arderne of Timperley Hall bequeathed 20 loads of turves a year to be cut on his part of Timperley Moss.

The area of Moss grew smaller as it was reclaimed for farming, and by the time the Bridgewater Canal was cut through in the late 18th century, the moss was divided up into small fields. Farmers from all over the township had one or two moss fields and a few new farms were established on the old moss land.

The area of Common was also enclosed and divided up, and a small hamlet grew up at the crossroads where Thorley Lane and Park Road meet Stockport Road, which was known as Four Lane Ends and now forms the centre of Timperley Village. Other farmhouses and cottages were scattered throughout the township, with most of them built along the main lanes, either singly or in small groups to form hamlets. The situation in Timperley remained much the same until the 1850s, and the map (right) shows some of the changes which had taken place by the 1870s.

The Manchester South Junction and Altrincham Railway was opened in 1849, followed by the Stockport, Timperley and Altrincham Junction, and terraced houses were built near Deansgate Lane and on Bloomsbury Lane. Larger houses were erected for merchants and businessmen, and land was also bought for this purpose by the merchants themselves. In the late 1850s Samuel Brooks, a Manchester banker, had bought several hundred acres of farmland in Timperley and planned to develop part of it for housing. He had two new roads constructed, one to connect Brooklands Station with Prospect House in Hale Barns, then called Hale Road, now better known as Brooks's Drive. The other road formed the basis for a new estate of large houses at Woodlands Park. Brooks died in 1864, but the Brooks Estate continued as a major landowner in Timperley until split up in the 1920s and 1930s.

The slow steady growth of Timperley up to the 1850s is shown in the population figures which increased from 588 in 1801 to 1008 in 1851, while the number of houses increased from 84 to 201. But in the next 20 years up to 1871, the population doubled again to 2112 and another 224 houses were built. After this period of rapid growth, the rate of increase slowed down until the 1930s when again the population almost doubled in 10 years.

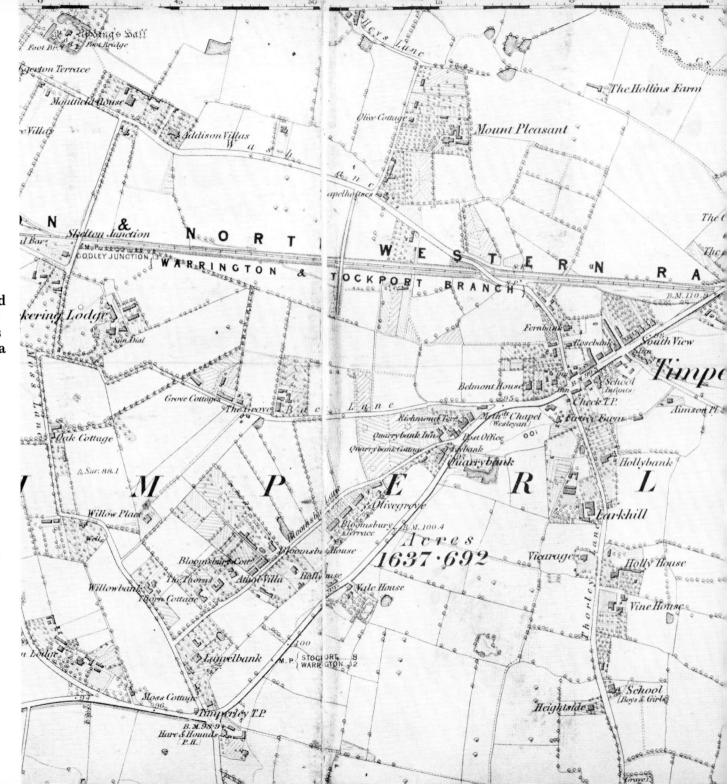

Timperley Hall

Known to many people as the Old Hall Hotel, and previously the Golf House Hotel, Timperley Hall probably dates from the late 18th century, and was built to replace the old hall which stood inside the moat at the rear. The old hall was possibly pulled down when the new one was built, as there is no trace of it on the large-scale Tithe map of 1838, and the area inside the moat was then used as a garden, as it is now.

The earliest reference to the Hall itself comes on the death of William Arderne in 1584, when his holdings included 8 other farms and a total of 378 acres, 200 being heathland. The hall and its lands, covering perhaps one quarter of Timperley, then passed by marriage to the Brereton family of Ashley, then to Sir Amos Meredith. In the mid 18th century it was acquired by George Johnson who left it to his son, the Rev. Croxton Johnson, Rector of Wilmslow. By the middle of the 19th century, the land was owned by James Wood, the Hall being occupied by Charles Pilling, gent., and Thomas Carr having the farmhouse at the back of the Hall and farming the 145 acres round about.

In 1883 the field on the corner of Wood Lane was leased to the Timperley Cricket Club, and in the 1890s the land immediately around the Hall was let to the Timperley Golf Club, along with the use of the Hall for a club house. In 1934 Altrincham Council bought the whole of Timperley Hall Farm from the owner Mr. F. A. Tomlinson, for the purpose of "Public Walks, Pleasure and Recreational Grounds", and the private golf course became a municipal one.

The buildings at the Hall included the farmhouse, then occupied by Mr. Hugh Bradbury the last farmer, two cottages, one of which housed the groundsman, Timothy Jepson, plus the usual barns and stables and an 'Irishman's shanty' or bothy. This was a small building where farm workers, often seasonal labourers, were housed. The old coach-house has been altered and is now part of the golf club house, and there must at one time have been a pigeon house to provide fresh meat in the winter, as the field on the right was called Dove House Field.

The Toll Bar

Opposite the Hare and Hounds on the corner of Stockport Road and Moss Lane, the Toll House was built when the Stockport and Warrington Turnpike Trust was set up in 1821, and was demolished when the tolls were abolished in 1880. Manchester Road, also known as 'Washway', had been a Turnpike Road since 1765, making part of the Chester to Manchester route. When the Trusts for the Stockport Road and Washway came to an end, the roads were returned to the care of the local council, when it was estimated that four men would be needed as manual labour to maintain the roads in Timperley. Previously the other roads in the township had been repaired when necessary using local labour, the payment in 1872 for working on the roads being 7 shillings (35p) a day for man, horse and cart, for the hours 7am to 12 noon and 2 till 6pm each day.

In 1919 the roads were described as "paved half the width (with stone setts), the other half ordinary macadam", i.e. crushed stone. The Census of 1851 shows the occupier of the 'Turnpike House' on Stockport Road as Samuel Jackson, with his wife and *ten* children, aged from 4 to 22. The site is now occupied by a petrol filling station, but the houses beyond are still standing. The one visible beyond the toll gate, called Ribblesdale, was the home of John Lambert, a staunch Methodist and Liberal who was Chairman of the Parish Council and a Councillor until his death in 1927.

Henry Staton, the last toll-keeper.

Railways

The construction of the Manchester South Junction and Altrincham Railway in 1849 was not without opposition locally, in fact a meeting of the ratepayers of Timperley agreed unanimously to oppose the building of any railways in the township. But it really only affected those with land in West Timperley and had less physical effect on the area than the Stockport, Timperley and Altrincham Junction, which was opened in 1866. This involved the demolition of several cottages on Park Road, and the crossing of three roads – Stockport Road, Park Road and Moss Lane – as well as the Canal. Also two gated crossings had to be made to allow access to farms off Park Road. One of these lanes, opposite Heyes Lane, was later altered to its present route over Stony Bridge to Grove Lane.

The railways brought added dangers of course: in 1890 one of the children from the Village School was killed "while playing under the arch over the railway line". The Stockport line later came under the control of the Cheshire Lines Committee and the two nearest stations on it were built in the typical style of C.L.C. stations. Both were on the edges of Timperley at Baguley and at West Timperley, on Manchester Road opposite to Jackson & Edwards Garage, where the railway cottages are still to be seen. Where the M.S.J. & A. R. and the Stockport line crossed near Deansgate Lane, quite an important junction developed, named after the owner of Pickering Lodge, John Skelton. In the 1940s Skelton Junction handled about five freight trains each way in an hour, including the familiar long lines of I.C.I. wagons carrying limestone to the chemical works near

Northwich. From 1879 the 'Timperley Curve' provided a direct link from the Stockport line to the M.S.J. & A.R., with a regular service from Stockport to Manchester Central Station, but this ended when the Curve was removed in 1903.

The Bridgewater Canal

The stretch of the Bridgewater Canal which passes through Timperley from Stretford to Runcorn was opened in 1776. It almost cut off the western part of the township and divided some farms into two parts, separated by only a few yards of water, but needing a much longer walk via Park Road bridge to reach fields on the other side. However the Canal much improved the transport of market garden and dairy produce into Manchester, and the supply locally of other goods including coal to a small wharf at Park Road bridge.

It also introduced what was known as 'Manure Traffic', when the night soil collected from the privies of Manchester was brought by barges, off-loaded onto the canal bank near Deansgate Lane and then carted to the fields to be spread as manure. Needless to say this produced various complaints from residents in Deansgate Lane! In 1895 there were 29 boats involved in the manure traffic at Carrington and Timperley. In many cases the crews, and sometimes their families, lived on their barges, and this also applied to the manure boats, where there was only a double wooden bulkhead between the cargo and living quarters.

Above: The "Baguley Bus", which provided a regular service from Stockport to Altrincham.

Left: A steam powered barge about 1910 heading towards Altrincham alongside a steam train pulling into Timperley Station. The barge on the left could well be carrying manure.

Park Road and Station Approach

The Canal and railways provided easier transport for fresh produce for the town dwellers in Manchester, which encouraged the growth of market gardening. But on the other hand, the mill owners and merchants moved away from the towns to the quiet of the countryside, so that Timperley acquired a number of large houses, referred to in contemporary directories as "Gothic villas" and "genteel residences". However most of these were built some distance away from the railways and the men travelling regularly into Manchester had to use either their own carriages or the local cabs. The plight of the cabmen waiting at Timperley Station in all weathers was recognised, and through the efforts of Miss Hattie Bell a wooden shelter was built and furnished with linoleum, a cooking stove, table and lockers.

The Pelican

The early history of the Pelican is not clear, but it may date from the time when the road was made a Turnpike in 1756. The tenants have changed quite often over the years and included one woman, Sarah Frank who was there in the 1830s and also farmed the 20 acres belonging to the pub. On Census day in 1851 the landlord, John Savage, had a salt dealer staying and incidentally the same hostler who had been there with Sarah Frank in 1841.

In the 1860s John Knowles was the publican and also a hay and straw dealer. It seems to have been a general thing that the pubs alone could not provide a living, and in most cases the publicans had a second occupation. For example in 1864, the tenants of the other pubs in Timperley included besides farmers, a blacksmith, a shoemaker and a wheelwright. Another tenant at the Pelican, James Seddon advertised himself as "The Farmer's Auctioneer" – cattle salesman, auctioneer and valuer. He was appointed one of the Guardians of the Poor for Timperley in 1889 but died the next year, and there were two more landlords before the arrival of Walter Bruton about 1905.

The ownership changed in 1926 and a few years later the new owners decided to put up a new building. This was built behind the old Pelican, which was then pulled down leaving the forecourt of the present hotel.

Wash Lane.   Timperley.

Left: The houses on the left, Egerton Terrace, could hardly be called Gothic villas but together with houses in 'Muir's Avenue', just before Brookfield Avenue, they formed a small group of larger houses, one being used as a ladies' school run by Robert Crawford. The tree on the right marks the entrance to Riddings Hall.

Trams and Buses

The tram service along Manchester Road began in 1906, with electric tramcars running every 10 minutes in the morning and every 7½ minutes in the evening until the last journey from Manchester at 10.30 pm, the fare being 4½d. (2p) for the 7½ mile trip. The trams reached Park Road, Timperley by August 17th, 1906 but it was another 9 months before they ran to the terminus at the Downs, Altrincham. The trams were replaced in 1931 by Manchester Corporation buses, but by then there was a well-established bus service in Timperley.

In 1922 the Timperley Bus Co. was started by Mr. Lister from a garage in Cow Lane, which later became the Gem Laundry. The company had two 20-seater Ford buses with solid tyres and the speed limit was then 12 mph. The first two drivers were Ronald Portman and Mr. G. L. Turner. The latter moved from a village near the Ford works in Lincolnshire in response to a need for someone familiar with Ford buses. He travelled by train up to Manchester, tram to Park Road junction, and then had the long walk up Park Road to the Village.

The service provided ran from the Stonemason's Arms via Park Road and along Moss Lane to the Hare and Hounds, then to Kingsway, Altrincham. In the other direction, the present Delaheys Road route terminated at Lloyd Street, but was later extended to the Bay Malton at Oldfield Brow, via Regent Road and Market Street. An extension was also made to Baguley Sanatorium via Roundthorn (Shady Lane).

The company was taken over in 1924 by the Altrincham and District Motor Bus Services

Ltd. (John Wood's company), with slightly smaller buses, and the Deansgate Lane route was extended down Brook Lane, over Navigation Crossings and along Grosvenor Road. (The Timperley Bus Co. was not allowed to run down Brook Lane because of the narrowness and sharp bends, and the size of the buses.)

The Altrincham and District was in its turn taken over by the North Western Road Car Co. Ltd. which had been running a service from Stockport to Altrincham via Timperley Village for the past three years.

Sample fares in 1929 were: From the Stonemason's Arms to Stockport 10d. and to Altrincham 3d. By 1931 it was even cheaper, the fare to Altrincham being 2d. (In 1963 the adult fare to Altrincham on the No. 71 or No. 80 was 8d. and 4d. for children.)

Above: The Old Pelican on Manchester Road, taken about 1910 while Walter Bruton was the landlord. The trams provided a new form of transport to replace the old horse omnibuses, but horsedrawn waggonettes were still very popular for outings, with canvas covers in case of rain. The trams were required to stop at the Pelican to 'clock-in' at the time-clock on the right of the picture.

Riddings Hall

The land belonging to Riddings Hall at one time stretched from the Canal almost to Heyes Lane and from Park Road to the Sale boundary. The Hall itself was situated near the Station, inside a wide moat approached over a stone bridge. The original hall was a fairly small building of timber framing with wattle and daub between, probably 15th century, which later had an extension added to one side.

The Riddings was apparently sold in 1498 by the Ardernes of Timperley Hall to Thomas Vaudrey. It remained with the Vaudrey family until about the 1630s when it was bought by Thomas Gerrard, who was later one of the defenders at the Siege of Wythenshawe Hall by Roundhead soldiers in 1643–44. Gerrard went to support the owner Robert Tatton, and was shot in the leg, not by the enemy, but by his own pistol which exploded accidentally. He survived this however and died in 1672 but had no male heirs and so was the last as well as the first Gerrard of Riddings. His story was used as the basis for a novel called "Sybilla" written by Mrs. G. Linnaeus Banks, author of "The Manchester Man".

After this the Riddings passed through different hands until the 19th century when it was owned by a family called Taylor. It was bought in the 1860s by John Keymer and he lived in a house which had been built in one of the fields opposite the end of Moss Lane – Moatfield House. The house was pulled down about 1900 but the gate posts remain.

The Riddings had been occupied during the 18th and 19th centuries by tenant farmers, and as it was the second largest farm (after Timperley Hall), the tenants were quite influential men. They included George Fletcher, one of the leaders of the Methodist congregation in Timperley in the mid 19th century and one of the township officers for nearly 20 years.

Mr. Thomas Garner was the last tenant to farm at Riddings Hall, and in 1933 the remaining fields were sold, although the house itself remained inside its moat until the 1960s. The grounds were later used by the Riddings Hall Social Club, whose new centre was opened in 1948 by the Mayor of Altrincham, Alderman Whitley, and which became a thriving social centre for the area. Besides being used as a nursery school, and a meeting room for various groups, Christmas shows and plays were performed by the drama section of the Club, and the building was also the venue for the Timperley 'Little Show' held by the Social Club, for garden flowers and produce, including preserves.

The site of the Hall is now occupied by the houses in Riddings Court, but its name and those of the families connected with it are preserved in some of the road names – Riddings, Arderne, Vaudrey, Gerrard, Leicester (the tenant at the turn of the century) and Garner.

Churches

Until the 1850s Timperley was included in the much larger Parish of Bowdon, which meant a trek on foot for most people each Sunday, up to St. Mary's Church at the end of The Firs or St. George's at Altrincham. However a thriving Methodist congregation in Timperley, had grown gradually from a few people meeting in the cottage of the leader Samuel Holt, which stood opposite the Vicarage in Thorley Lane. This soon became too small and in 1833 a chapel was built on land bought from John Marsland, at the corner of Heyes Lane and Park Road. The chapel has always been assumed to be the three cottages adjoining Constable's shop, but on the Tithe Map of 1838 the chapel was the only building on that corner and was shown further back from the road. It was a very small building, the whole plot of chapel and yard being only 330 square yards. It is possible it may have been the building on the right, set back from the cottages, which had a Gothic arched window over the door, and did not look like one of the typical local cottages.

The Methodist Society continued to grow and Heyes Lane Chapel also became too small so a new chapel was built on Stockport Road and opened in 1847. The chapel was largely altered in 1883 when the roof height was raised and a gallery added, and the school-room at the rear was extended in 1897. This second chapel was replaced in 1938 by the present Methodist Church, and in recent years the old building was used as a hemming factory until 1982.

The story of Timperley Methodism was recorded in 1933 by Ernest H. Wright, the Minister at that time, in a small book which showed how certain families had been important in its growth. It is not possible to name them all here, but one family had a great effect both in the Methodist church and in Timperley generally. Before about 1840 the name Jackson was not common in Timperley, but about that time Samuel and Mary Jackson came to live at the Toll House, then moved to Bridge Farm near Stockport Road railway bridge. They both became Methodists, taking active part in the local congregation, and raised their eleven children as Methodists. The six sons all had large families and for some time the chapel at Heyes Lane was known as "Jackson's Chapel", and today many local people can claim a relationship to the Jacksons.

Below: Park Road, known as Wash Lane until about the 1930s, was obviously not troubled by traffic when this view was taken.

Christ Church

The sight of the new Methodist Chapel in 1847 may have been the final incentive for the movement to have a Church and Vicarage erected in Timperley. The main organisers were Benjamin Bagnall of the Oaklands, Wood Lane, and John Skelton of Pickering Lodge, and the site for the church was given by Mr. John Barratt of Altrincham. The foundation stone was laid on the 13th November 1848 and the church was opened less than a year later in September 1849, although the new Parish of Christ Church Timperley was not formed until May 1852. The land for a Vicarage was given by Mrs. Nathaniel Taylor and the first Vicar was the Rev. Edward Dowling.

The Church was soon found to be too small for the growing population and in 1865 it was extended to its present size by the addition of transepts, the chancel, organ chamber and vestry, the seating being increased from 497 to about 800. One third of the seating was free, but for the rest, pew rents were charged and the better-off members of the congregation paid for the use of the same pew each week, some having their names added and fitments such as boxes for prayer books. The church was originally plastered inside, but in 1888 this was replaced by the terra cotta walling which is still intact.

Not only was Christ Church extended, but the continuing growth of population in the Parish also led to the establishment of two chapels to cope with increased numbers.

The Parish of Timperley still includes parts of Baguley and Hale, and St. David's Church on Grove Lane in Hale was built for the benefit of people moving into new housing in the Hermitage area. It was originally intended to be a separate parish, and until a new parish church could be built a temporary one was erected, and dedicated on 20 August 1914. However, the First World War intervened and the plans for neither the new parish nor the new church were carried out.

The people in the Deansgate Lane area had the benefit of services held in St. Andrew's Mission School, after it was opened in 1883, but had to wait until 1929 before St. Andrew's Church was built.

The Roman Catholics were later in establishing a church in Timperley with the building of St. Hugh of Lincoln Church, opened on Sunday 13th December 1931. This was also built as a temporary church, and has now been replaced by the new St. Hugh's, opened exactly 50 years later.

Drawing of the church pre 1865.

Below: This view shows the pulpit in its original position, and the intricate paintwork on the ceiling. It was taken probably about 1930 and shows the electric pendant lights which replaced the gas lighting in 1920.

Schools

With the closure of both the Village School and St. Andrew's School in Deansgate Lane in 1981, there ended a period of at least 200 years in which education in Timperley had been provided under the influence of the Church of England.

In 1789 a school was built on Stockport Road opposite the junction with Bedford Drive, and in 1802 Miss Jane Houghton of Baguley gave an endowment to "the public school at Timperley" for the teaching of poor children from Timperley and Baguley, who were to be selected by the Curate at St. George's Altrincham. In 1859 there were 14 free scholars, while the other local children paid their "School Pence", literally one penny a week.

The school became too small for the numbers attending and in 1855 a new school was built in Thorley Lane and the older children were transferred there, leaving the infants at the old school. The present Infants' School on Stockport Road was built in 1873 to replace the original school, which was then converted into two cottages known as "Thompson Villa", and was finally demolished about 1969.

Thorley Lane School

Built on land given by Lord Stamford, the Mixed School in Thorley Lane had separate entrances for Girls and Boys, with a schoolhouse at the rear. From 1874 this was occupied by Mr. Charles Fitton, who was headmaster there until his retirement in 1917. In those 43 years he taught hundreds of local children, many of whom kept in touch by visits and letters, as they did also with his daughter Miss Edith Fitton, who took over as head for a short time after her father's retirement. Miss Fitton took an active part in local affairs, especially in education and local government, being made an Alderman of Altrincham Borough and its first lady Mayor. Her brother Edmund Fitton was the photographer who produced the "Nottif" series of local postcards.

Above left: Thompson Villa; The upper floor at Thompson Villa included a Reading Room, but was also used for classes, and in 1865 a boy fell from the upper window, but was not seriously injured.

Above right: Thorley Lane. The Mixed School stood on the site now occupied by Christ Church Hall, and the house in the distance is Glendaruel, next door to St. John the Baptist Roman Catholic Church, which was opened in 1960. The ivy round the door and windows of the school was periodically cut by one of the pupils, with the payments appearing in the official accounts.

School photographs were first taken in Timperley in 1875, but this one dates from 1915 and shows Miss Edith Fitton with one of her two classes at Thorley Lane School. The names of the class have been recalled by one member and sound like a roll-call of local families. From the back, from right to left: Steve Hodgkinson, Jack Dean, Bill Stiles, Bob Rogerson, Louis Denton, Jack Bradburn, Laurie Tyler, –, Lewis Jackson. 2nd row: Freda Kelsall, Willie Gilligan, Mary Mitchell, Bessie Kayswell, Marion Rutter, Peggy Barker. 3rd row: – Garner, Ada Barrow, Marie Evans, Amy Graves, – Hulme, Jessie Fowler, Eva Pilling. 4th row: Ken Smith, Wilf McGuinness, George Gresty, Arthur Bunnell, Jack Coldwell, Ted Hulme, George Hale, Arthur Kelsall, Bernie Jones, Harold Jones, Percy Renshaw, Jack Keogh, –.

Lark Hill School

Besides the Church schools in Timperley there have also been a number of private schools, although many only existed for a few years, for example Elizabeth Lawson in 1888 was running a school in the first house on the left of the old Methodist Chapel on Stockport Road. In 1916 only two were listed in Slater's Directory, Robert Crawford's "ladies' school" at Egerton Terrace in Park Road, and Miss Mary Adshead at Lark Hill. In 1914 she had moved her ladies' school from a house called Sherwood on Stockport Road near the Quarry Bank, to Lark Hill in Thorley Lane, with its beautiful landscaped grounds including an ornamental pool and bridge in the style of the "Willow Pattern". An advertisement of 1914 offered "Elocution Classes for Children and Adults conducted by Miss Morden Grey". The school came to an end in 1920 with the death of Miss Adshead, and Lark Hill reverted to a private house. (It had been the home of James Kay from the 1880s until 1911.) The house and grounds were bought by Altrincham Council in 1947, when many of the trees were felled, Thorley Lane widened, the house demolished and the grounds finally became the present public park.

In later years there were other private schools, at Brookfield House on Park Road, run by Mrs. Beedle, and one in Heyes Lane, but the only one still in existence is the Forest School, on Moss Lane, founded in 1924 by the Misses Clegg in the house called Oak Cottage, and run for several years recently by Mr. and Mrs. Hoogewerf.

Below: The lawn at Lark Hill, with Thorley Lane on the left. The young lady with the tennis racquet is Mary Leather (now Mrs. Barber).

Fir Tree Farm

The area now occupied by the Village was a part of Timperley Common and it was probably divided up in the late 17th century, when several 'black and white' timber-framed houses were erected. One of these was Fir Tree Farm, built by Humphrey Paulden in 1676, and it remained in the Paulden family until about 1860.

Like many local examples, the timber framing was built on top of a low wall made of large sandstone blocks. The house was demolished to make way for the Co-op stores, built in 1928, but some of the stone blocks remain to make up the wall fronting the car park on Thorley Lane.

Many families now living in Timperley and round about are connected with old farming families such as the Heywoods, Hulmes, Garners, Jacksons, Warburtons, Whiteleggges, Thorpes, Rogersons and Roberts.

The local family connections become very complicated, especially when seven or eight children was a common number. The tenants of Fir Tree Farm provide a good example.

In the late 19th century the tenant was Robert Rogerson, who married one of the daughters of Samuel and Mary Jackson. One of the Rogerson daughters married Thomas Roberts, a grandson of James and Mary Whitelegge. He moved from Bloomsbury Lane in 1914 to take over Fir Tree Farm, and moved on later to Fox Farm in Brook Lane, one of his daughters marrying a Jackson. And so on!

Mr. and Mrs. Thomas Roberts.

Left: Fir Tree Farm

Right: Stockport Road. This was taken before 1909 when the Manchester and County Bank bought the land including the butcher's shop occupied by Charles J. Skelton, and built the Bank, now the National Westminster. The butcher's later became Percy Rook's shop.

The position of Fir Tree Farm can be seen on the right, set back from the road with the thatched building in front. The sandstone wall ran from the corner of Thorley Lane along the length of Stockport Road to the Hare and Hounds, following the bend in the road here so that it appears more exaggerated than at present where we now have the wide forecourts in front of the shops in Mayfield Buildings.

STOCKPORT ROAD

The Village

The Village.

Timperley

Left: Four Lane Ends and the 'Big Tree'. The crossroads in the Village, about 1910, showing the 'Big Tree' at the corner of Park Road, and Mrs. Renwick's shop on the corner of the old Stonemason's Arms. The big beech tree was reputed to be 250 years old, but despite a petition signed by 364 residents and a letter to the Guardian by George Faulkner Armitage, it was cut down in 1924 on the grounds of danger to pedestrians and to motor traffic.

The sign post points down Park Road for Manchester as the most direct route, the present alternative of Princess Parkway not being built until much later. The

fence by the Big Tree enclosed the grounds of Holly House the home of Mr. Bannister.

Above: The Village and the Church Inn. Really a typical small country inn, the Church Inn had a garden at the rear on Thorley Lane, where rustic benches and tables were set out, with trellis work around the back door as well as the front. Like most of the other pubs the tenants changed fairly often, but in this case the pub itself was changed and after the publican Frank Taylor left it had only two more years before 1915 when Isaac Webb

moved with his greengrocer's business from two doors away. He was followed by Kendricks and later it was closed for a time and then occupied by A. E. Pryor & Sons. Mr. Pickston then took over and moved with his business when the old building was demolished and Charles Court erected in its place.

Between the Church Inn and Woodall's off-licence next door, was a wooden hut originally occupied by a cobbler, and then by a joiner, Mr. Buckley. The inventor of the dye used for marking sheep known as "raddle", was a Mr. Drinkwater who lived at Woodalls.

Below: Baker Street going off to the right was the only 'street' in Timperley, all the others being roads, lanes, groves, etc. It was also previously known as "The Barracks" and was a short street with terraced houses on both sides, Leather's grocer's shop on one corner, shown here, and Harry Barker's smithy on the other (now the site of the new branch library).

The next street along towards the Stonemason's, Orchard Place, had houses on the one side only, with Mr. Hankinson's coalyard on the other. Orchard Place was also known as "Duck Street", but this was a nickname, acquired because of a man who kept ducks at the end of the street.

Open Air Services were held on Sunday evenings in the summer months at various locations: July 1889 saw them at Baker Street, Orchard Place, Grove Lane (probably at the Y.M.C.A. Institute) and at Baguley. The following year brought the addition of an "American Organ" which was carried through the streets to the services, which were very popular.

Further entertainment was provided by the Parish Room and Club, on the left with the turret. This was opened in 1910, a season ticket for the bowling green costing then 3/6d. (17½p). Tennis courts were added later and in 1927 the subscription was 15/- (75p) for gentlemen players and 10/6d. (52½p) for ladies. The "Dangerous Cross Roads" sign in front of the Village Farm was put up in 1916 by the Manchester Automobile Club at the request of the Parish Council.

Timperley Parish Nurse

The Parish Nurse Fund was started by the Church in 1888, and by 1935 had grown to become the Timperley and Baguley District Nursing Association. It provided a valuable service to the community, for example in 1904–5, Nurse Jackson made 1,744 visits (by bicycle), and cases attended included hysteria, epilepsy, sciatica, gout, cancer, mumps, dropsy, jaundice, whitlow, shingles, consumption, bronchitis and convulsions. There have actually been very few nurses over the years; Mrs. Fanny Jackson was appointed in 1899 and retired in 1927, when her place was taken by Nurse Miller who retired in 1953.

Village Farm

Situated between Bedford Drive and Aimson Road on the site now occupied by Vantage Garages, the Village Farm was also known as Four Lane Ends Farm, and several local families have farmed there.

Henry Booth came to the farm in the 1890s. and took an active part in village life, being a Parish Councillor from 1906 to 1919. His son Harry became a butcher, with a business in Deansgate Lane, while two daughters married two sons of Hugh Bradbury of Timperley Hall Farm. The Village Farm was a part of Samuel Brooks's estate and it came up for sale at the same time as Manor Farm in 1924. It was then being farmed by the Bradburys as a dairy farm, and it continued as one when the Woods family took over. It was finally demolished about 1940.

Inset: Mrs. Mary Woods in the farmyard. The building at the back was the Gem Laundry in Cow Lane.

Below: The front of the Village Farm with Mrs. Woods at the gate. The "quick service" was provided by boot repairer Billy Thompson, and further on the left was Jack Shearman's Garage.

The Stonemason's Arms

The Stonemason's Arms has changed somewhat from the public house first built in 1840. The first landlord and probable owner was John Arnold, stonemason, who had previously been at the Church Inn across the road, and it was known then as the 'Mason's Arms'. When John died in the 1840s his eldest son William took over the pub, while his widow and other three sons, all of them masons, moved elsewhere. The youngest, Uriah Arnold, later had a stonemason's business at the premises now Jackson's Garage on Stockport Road.

From about 1860 the Stonemason's was run by James and then Maggie Platt. At the same time the stabling at the pub was being used by Charles Fletcher, who owned and hired out carriages and horses from "the Stone Mason's Arms Yard".

The good stabling was a feature of the Stonemason's and was advertised in 1896 along with the bowling green as an attraction for outings. The pub also had its own vines. The stables were used during the First World War for Army horses when any cavalry troops were passing through. The landlord during the War was Jack Atherton who came to the pub in 1906. He was a District Councillor in 1913 and a founder member of the 'Timperley Lodge' of Freemasons, founded in 1911.

In 1926 the owners, Hardy's Crown Brewery Ltd. (Samuel Hardy lived at Pickering Lodge), applied to the Parish Council for permission to rebuild the pub completely. Objections were raised by the local Councillors, with comments about city gin palaces, and the plans were altered to make the new frontage more in the style of the old one. During the rebuilding, the little shop on the corner of the pub, Mrs. Martha Renwick's Fancy Repository, was removed and the business transferred to the other side of the pub and was later run for many years by Mrs. Annie Farrell as 'The Corner Shop'.

Above: A family group on the bowling green at the Stonemason's, with on the right Mr. Jack Atherton, his sister and niece and another sister on the left. In the centre is Mrs. Atherton with her daughter Alice, and on the back row from the left, Mr. Edward Gresty, Mr. John Yates, blacksmith, and Mr. James Whitfield, the last two being neighbours on Stockport Road.

Right: The pub was more often known by its nick-name 'The Naked Child', which came from the stone plaque above the door, probably carved as an example of the mason's art, showing chisels, a mason's hammer and square rule as well as the child.

The Oaklands

Cloverley House

On the opposite side of Wood Lane, Cloverley House stood at the end of a long drive. It was built about 1860, and was included in that part of the Brooks estate sold in 1924. At that time the gardens included a tennis lawn, and a walled kitchen garden, with a conservatory and vinery. The tenant Mr. John L. Welch had the benefit of nine bedrooms, and a billiard room, and the outbuildings included a stable and coach-house, coachman's cottage, and a laundry.

Other large houses on Wood Lane included Oak Mount, the home of Sir Bosdin Thomas Leech, the Chairman of Manchester Waterworks Committee, a J.P. and a Parish Councillor. He died in 1912, but in the 1940s another J.P., Mrs. Bernard Williams lived there and in 1948 sold the house to the local branch of the Church of England Temperance Society and it became a probation hostel, equipped with a football pitch, gymnasium, joiner's shop and chapel, and was re-named Parkfield.

The Oaklands

Lincoln Drive and Wingate Drive now occupy the land which formed the grounds of the Oaklands on Wood Lane. The landscaped grounds included an L-shaped lake. In 1841 the house was owned by John Kaye a cabinet maker, who lived there with his family and three female servants. Ten years later it was the home of Benjamin Bagnall, who was influential in the building of the Parish Church. About 1880 George Faulkner, the editor of 'Bradshaw's Journal' lived at the Oaklands, and a regular visitor there was the author Mrs. G. Linnaeus Banks. (Note the road named after him – Faulkner Drive, on the opposite side of Wood Lane.) The Gothic ruins in the grounds were claimed to have been brought from Manchester Cathedral during reconstruction.

Belmont House

John Arnold, grandson of the man who first had the Stonemason's Arms, became a well-known auctioneer and valuer, starting the Altrincham Smithfield Market, held at the rear of the Unicorn Hotel in Altrincham. He was a prominent member of the community, being first a Parish Councillor from 1899, then a member of the Bucklow Rural District Council, one of the Guardians of the poor for Timperley, a County Councillor and Justice of the Peace. He was also a strong Conservative and active as President or Chairman of several local societies. From 1907 until his death in 1929 he lived at 'Belmont' on Stockport Road, which stood about where the present Methodist Schoolrooms are. The house was used as a Sunday school by the Church for many years.

Belmont House

Pickering Lodge

Pickering Lodge house was built in about 1850 for John Skelton (from Pickering, Yorkshire) and was later owned by George Hardy, of Hardy's Crown Brewery.

In 1915 it became the annexe to the Auxilliary Military Hospital at Heyesleigh, in Heyes Lane, the home of Dr. Louis Savatard. Heyesleigh Hospital was run by the Red Cross and started in 1914 with 15 beds. The number was increased to 36 when Pickering Lodge was lent by Sam Hardy, and the addition of a marquee in the grounds at Heyesleigh and a hut at Pickering Lodge brought the number of beds up to a total of 98.

The Hospitals were helped out by local donations in kind, as well as local volunteers, one scheme being the Church Lads Brigade Egg Collection. Up to the end of July 1916, the lads had collected 6,660 eggs from local farmers and householders, with Privates Leslie Heywood and H. Lauri only missing one day between them.

Another collection organised during the First World War was done by school children in 1917, when they collected horse chestnuts. These were to be used as a substitute for grain in an industrial process. They were to be collected in baskets and then addressed to: The Director of Propellant Supplies, Ministry of Munitions!

Part of Pickering Lodge Estate was sold for housing in 1920, and the house was finally bought by the council, found to be infested with dry rot and demolished. The grounds now contain tennis courts, bowling green and the entrance lodge at the corner of Grove Lane.

Moss Lane, Timperley.

Left: These cottages stood on the site of the Moss Trooper Hotel, and in the mid 19th century two separate small farms were run from them. Newstead Terrace is just off to the right, and the stone wall opposite is the boundary of the grounds belonging to Pickering Lodge.

Below: Pickering Lodge

11

The Hare and Hounds

The public house we know as the Hare and Hounds has had an interesting history, not always as a pub. It was owned by the Goulden family in the 18th century and possibly earlier, as there had been Gouldens in Timperley since at least 1620. When Richard Goulden died in 1767 he left a farm, then called 'Gouldens of the Mossend', to his son William, who was a weaver, and the house then included a Loom-house. He left his wife Ann the use of the parlour and the chamber over it, the kitchen garden, pump, close hedge (clothes hedge) and house of ease (privy).

The farmhouse probably became a pub in the early 19th century, although still owned by the Gouldens, who continued to farm the land. From the 1830s when John Chorlton was the landlord, it became an important meeting place, the Township Meetings being held there for a period, with suitable refreshment supplied. Much later the Timperley Prize Band used the old Dutch barn for their practices, and several local tradesmen stabled their van horses there.

Left: This was taken on the Cricket Ground, with the Hare and Hounds in the background, and dates from 1895, the occasion being a cricket match. The only person identified, third from left on the front row, was Sam Hallam, who married Sarah, the daughter of Joseph Knowles of Vale House.

Right: Looking in two directions along Stockport Road opposite the Hare and Hounds, about 1910.

In the upper photograph, Moss Lane is on the left and the turning to Wood Lane on the right, Shaftesbury Avenue not yet even thought of. It must have been a hot day, with both driver and horse wearing hats.

The building on the left belonging to Peter Rowlinson is seen better in the view below, which shows it as the Stockport Road Laundry. It was later run by Ernest Neild, but still known as Rowlinson's Laundry.

The buildings at the back were the works of Cross and Bell, joiners, builders and contractors. Both partners lived at Woodleigh, on Stockport Road just beyond their timber yard on the other side of Moss Lane. The firm was later taken over by John Collier.

There were other laundries in Timperley, one in Grove Lane in the cottages known as 'Potts' Cottages', run by Mrs. Vernon and later Wettenalls, and another off Wood Lane. This was a much larger affair run by the Brook Steam Laundry Co. Ltd. and employing about 40 people in 1900. In June 1900 it was severely damaged by fire, the Fire Brigade at Altrincham being contacted by telephone from Cloverley House, after the fire was discovered at 2 am. The laundry and contents were destroyed, but the company planned to rebuild, although in the meantime the 40 employees were out of work. However the laundry was not rebuilt and the land was taken over as a nursery.

Cloverley House

Vale Cottages

In the 19th century there were no buildings between the Hare and Hounds corner and the Quarry Bank, apart from Vale Cottages, and Vale House opposite. The cottages, originally four, date from the early 1800s. The right hand two were demolished in 1971 and the remaining two cottages were made into one.

Vale House, opposite, was occupied about 1900 by the Knowles family, which included William Knowles, shoemaker and repairer. The houses beyond Vale Cottages in this picture, built just before 1900, housed the Parish Clerk, Frank Bell junior, his father Francis T. Bell, collector of taxes, William Rook the schools' attendance officer, and Richard Shoesmith, the professional golfer at Timperley Golf Club.

Bloomsbury Lane

Bloomsbury Lane like several other roads in Timperley was previously known by another name. As Aimson Road used to be Cow Lane and Grove Lane was called Back Lane, Bloomsbury Lane was Deputy Lane.

Looking from the Quarry Bank Inn towards Moss Lane, almost the whole of the left side was occupied by terraces of houses built between the 1860s and 1890s, with one or two large houses at the Moss Lane end. One of these, Herbert Vale, was for a time the home of J. Edgar Webb J.P. The first house on the left was the home of coal dealer Aaron Smith, across the road from his depot. The residents of Bloomsbury Terrace included, in 1916, John Weaver, lamplighter. Gas mains had first been laid in Timperley in 1864 by the Altrincham Gas Co. and by this time Timperley had almost 200 gas lamps. Later, the lamplighter for the Village lived in Baker Street. His name was Teddy Benson, but he was known as 'Weskitt', because his first question on receiving his uniform in the Army was "Isn't there a waistcoat?".

Below: This view shows Park Road at the present junction with Dudley Road, the thatched building on the left belonging to Lime Tree Farm, then run by John Jackson as a market garden. Opposite was the market garden of Walter Fry, previously Alfred Rogerson's, and beyond that the Jubilee Recreation Ground. This was bought by public subscription to celebrate Queen Victoria's Diamond Jubilee in 1897. Over the next five years the 'Rec' was provided with swings (separate sets for boys and girls with bushes between) and seats, and was surrounded with trees planted by the Parish Councillors. Samuel Cottrell was appointed caretaker at a wage of 5/- a week in summer and 2/6 in winter. The ground was let for the pasturage of cows in the first year, but this was found to be highly unsuitable and the next year the grass was cut and sold as fodder!

The house with the black and white gates in the centre is now Hamer's Garage and was the home of 'Timperley Coachways'.

Deansgate Lane

This suburban scene (left) gives no hint of the industrial activity at the far end of Deansgate Lane. The road, which previously connected with Attenbury's Lane, was cut by the canal in the 18th century and then crossed by three railway lines, the level crossing nearest the canal having since been removed. The increased transport facilities provided by the canal and railways brought more industry. In the 19th century Ambler and Brooks' Tannery stood where Houldsworth Avenue is, and the British Mat Company's works occupied the left side of Deansgate Lane against the canal bank, until completely destroyed by fire in December 1927. The blaze attracted a crowd of about 300 people who stayed for 2 or 3 hours until after midnight, despite a keen frost which froze the hoses.

Many of the houses in the Deansgate area date from the late 19th century. The two terraces in Hall Avenue, 'Prospect Place' and 'Dean Terrace' both date from about 1860, and for the next 50 years, the road was known as Dean Terrace, until 1910 when the name was changed to Prospect Place.

Penny Bank

The Timperley Penny Savings Bank was started in 1881, and the community in the Deansgate area was sufficient to warrant a separate branch, which lasted until 1926. A site for a school had been acquired by the Parish in 1873, but the building was not started until 1882. Once opened, St. Andrew's Mission School on the corner of St. Andrew's Avenue became a centre for social events as well as doubling as a mission church, with a thriving Sunday School. In 1895 a Working Men's Reading Room was inaugurated in a room lent by Mr. T. Ambler and opened 5 nights a week.

Posy Row

At one time the occupiers of these seven cottages off Brook Lane included five families called Berry, although not all related! The cottages were built at different times, as can be seen in the change of brickwork between the first and second pair, with the three at the end added later. All were finished by 1838, when the tenants included 2 gardeners, a sawyer and a joiner. In 1916 one cottage was occupied by a camera maker (probably employed at Thornton-Pickards in Atlantic Street, makers of photographic equipment). A railway porter, Edwin Chadderton, lived in the middle house of the three and later became the Station Master at Timperley Station. His wife Mrs. Eliza Jane Chadderton is pictured (right) at the cottage door, and the other view (above) taken in the 1950s includes Mrs. Jessie Stone and her son Charles. Henley Drive now stands on the site of the cottages, which faced across to St. Andrew's Church and were demolished in 1963.

Mrs. Jessie Stone and family, Posy Row

Mrs. Eliza Jane Chadderton, Posy Row

Timperley Village.

Stockport Road

Taken in the 1930s, this photograph (opposite page) shows several well-known businesses, one of which, Mr. Frank Gibson's butcher's shop, is still operating from the same shop. The Post Office was transferred to Miss Mary Cockayne's draper's shop in 1915, and later run for several years by Mr. and Mrs. Matt Kelly.

Knowles's shoe shop was started by William Knowles, who made and repaired shoes in George Street, Altrincham, while his wife sold shoes from this shop. The sweet shop on the corner of Orchard Place was run by Mrs. Cross, who in the winter also sold hot drinks at 1d. a glass. The shop was later run by Mr. Reggie Lamb, who also loaned novels from a circulating library, as did the Post Office.

Circulating libraries had been provided in Timperley since 1897, when Miss Thompson opened a branch of the 'Modern Circulating Library of the Latest Novels of the Best Authors', along with magazines such as Strand, Chambers' Journal, Good Works, The Argosy, Woman at Home, and Girls' Own Paper. The charge for magazines was 1d. for 3 days, and for books 2d. from 4 to 7 days. the commercial lending libraries like these continued well after the council branch library was opened on Park Road in 1937.

Beyond Orchard Place was a row of houses and then Thompson Villa, the old school. Mr. George Hankinson had the end house with a door onto Orchard Place, and his coal yard at the rear, and in the same block were John Davenport, decorator and 'Auntie Nellie' Woodall. In Thompson Villa were the

Coldwells, and Thomas Bunnell, chauffeur for the Dyson family at Brook House, on Brooks's Drive. Next door was Eli Whiley cab proprietor, then another shop and Mr. Leather's grocer's on the corner of Baker Street, with the Tanzaro advert. Opposite the end of Baker street was the Railway Inn.

Above: Thorley Lane
Stockport Road and Thorley Lane junction taken about 1950. The old Church Inn on the left then occupied by Pryor's Greengrocer and Fishmonger, with the side of Percy Rook's shop showing the old butcher's slaughter-house at the rear. The bus stop on the left was by Billy Rodney's wooden hut where he did shoe repairs, which stood in the garden of the Church Inn. In the other direction the bus stop was opposite the side door of the Stonemason's Arms.

Inset, opposite page:
Percy S. Rook in his shop on the corner of Thorley Lane. He moved there from the shop now Terry's gown shop, which was previously occupied by his father William Rook, known to local children as 'Daddy Rook', the schools' attendance officer. Like his father, Percy was interested in local affairs, being a Parish Councillor, and serving from 1907 until the amalgamation of Timperley with Altrincham in 1936.

The shop then was a fascinating place, with ranks of little wooden drawers of nails, screws and washers, tools hanging up and bins in the back and in the yard containing paraffin, fertilisers, etc. He was nearly always seen in a long brown overall, and his stock answer if something was not available was that it was at Baguley Station waiting to be picked up. With him in this photograph is the late Mr. Ronnie Bowden, who was a hard worker for disabled people, and learned the deaf and dumb sign language so that he could talk to everyone.

The Railway Inn

The Railway Inn occupied the vacant piece of land at the corner of Aimson Road now used by Vantage Garage for car parking. It was built around the 1860s, but later extended and altered about 1926, by which time it was owned by Boddingtons. For the last 30 years of the 19th century, the landlord was Benjamin Haigh. Mrs. Ann Greaves took over from him about 1908, as beerseller and it was still licensed for beer only when this photo (left) was taken in the late 1940s, the licensee being Alfred Hertzog.

Left: This was taken before an outing to Blackpool Lights, and among the group are Mary Heywood and Mrs. Heywood, Mr. and Mrs. Jeffery, their son and daughter Margaret, Mary Hale, Ethel Ostick, Mrs. Callaghan, John Heneghan, George Hale.

Brook's Drive

The toll house at the end of Brooklands Road, by the roundabout, belonged to the Brooks estate, and tolls were charged for travelling along Brooklands Road, with a weighbridge just outside the tollhouse.

Samuel Lamb and his family lived at the Toll Bar Cottage from about 1860 until 1926, when his wife died and he moved to Altrincham Road, Baguley, but was only there a short time before he also died. He was the sexton at Christ Church from 1882 to 1919, and had been a member of the choir there for over 40 years.

Manor Farm

Until the 1860s Sugar Lane (now Ridgeway Road) ended at Manor Farm, and branched into a lane leading in front of the house to the fields beyond. When Samuel Brooks bought the farm along with others in Timperley in 1857, he made great changes. The layout of the farm was altered and new buildings constructed, and a large extension built onto the end of the farmhouse. Sugar Lane was continued straight past the farm to the junction with Brooks's Drive.

In the 1880s, it was farmed by Joseph Cooper Rogerson, who died in 1891 and it was then taken by James Austin, and the family remained at Manor Farm until 1974. By the time the farm changed owners in 1924 it had grown from 50 to 150 acres. It was then described as a model farm, with a stable for 9 horses, shippon for 20 cows, and various other buildings including a 'Paddyhouse'. It was quite common for farms to provide bothies or shanties for seasonal Irish labourers, hence the 'Paddy' house.

The farm now belongs to the Civil Service Sports Club and the farm buildings have been converted to include squash courts, showers and other facilities.

Top right: The barns on the left of this postcard originally were part of Sugar Lane Farm, and were later bought and used by Austin & Percival, Agricultural Motor and General Engineers.

The Austins had no less than three huge steam powered threshing machines, which were hired out over a large area of north-east Cheshire.

The fields between Ridgeway Road and Clay Lane now are mainly occupied by sports grounds, including the Civil Service Club and the Silver Wings Club, and this follows a tradition of nearly 100 years of use of the Manor Farm fields for recreation. In 1893 James Austin allowed the Church Sunday School the use of a field for the annual treat, and this continued for several years, with the occasional retreat to a barn in case of showers. The fields were also used in the 1930s when Cobham's Flying Circus visited Timperley, giving flights to local people for 5/- a flip.

Below right: Mr. Ken Austin beside the Gipsy Moth in which Amy Johnson flew to Australia. The field used was at the end of Fairfield Road, and later became known as the show ground for the Timperley Horse and Horticultural Society.

Farming Background

While some of the farms in Timperley continued with crops and livestock, many small farmers turned to market gardening from the early 19th century, and until the growth in house building from the 1930s onwards, both farming and market gardening were very important in the area.

In 1864 the introduction to Timperley in Kelly's Directory comments that "very large quantities of strawberries are grown here", and references were made in later years to onions and carrot seed, while of course there is a variety of rhubarb called 'Timperley Early'. Rhubarb was also known locally as 'Baguley Beef' and was one of several crops grown locally. The strawberries mentioned in 1864 were still being grown at Fox Farm, Brook Lane in 1904 when a fire in the loft over the stables almost destroyed a large number of strawberry baskets. Another fire at John Warburton's market garden on Wood Lane in 1925 burnt out, besides a stable and shed, a glasshouse containing hundreds of tomato plants. However there were still farms growing wheat, and providing milk and beasts for meat, and when new houses were erected on Stockport Road between the Quarry Bank and Vale House, in the 1930s, they still backed on to corn fields, complete with corncrakes.

Some of the market gardens doubled as nurseries, often producing bedding plants for sale. There have also been larger firms of nurserymen and seedsmen including Samuel Yates down Heyes Lane, (and now at Macclesfield), Clibrans at Delaheys Farm and on the land now taken by Peter Yates' Garden Centre, and Dickson, Brown and Tait, seedsmen, still in Attenbury's Lane.

Timperley Show

The Timperley Horse and Horticltural Society was started in 1945, the aim being "to provide clean and healthy entertainment, at the same time promoting and encouraging civic pride among all sections of Timperley's community, young and old". The officers of the Society in the first year included Edgar Webb as President, plus Frank Gibson, Frank Britton, Wilf Mercer, Arthur Crosby and Arthur Beattie.

Left top: This photo taken at the show in 1950 includes (L to R) W. Godsell, Wilf Bendell and Eddie Pryor warming up with hot soup.

Left below: Local growers competed at shows sometimes many miles away. More local is this prize-winning display of vegetables by Mr. Lewis Garner at Wythenshawe Show.

Timperley Prize Band

The Timperley Brass Band was formed in 1909, with a number of local people subscribing to pay for instruments and uniforms. For several years a music festival was held on the Jubilee Recreation Ground in aid of the District Nurse Fund. The president and vice-president for the first year were John Arnold and John Lambert, two well-known personalities, but the rest of the officers were drawn from among the bandsmen, with H. Jackson as secretary, Charles Taylor, treasurer for many years, and J. H. Pearson, the leader and conductor.

Right: Members of the band included Billy Rodney, Bob Whitfield, Jim Saynor, Harry Fleet, Jimmy Laurie, Jack Litherland, and Jack Warrington. The occasion here was probably Christ Church Rose Queen Festival; Mr. Pearson seated at the left.

Rose Queen Festivals

The first Rose Queen Festival at Christ Church in 1948 was typical of many Timperley church events, when all the local families joined in to enjoy the day. That first year it was held on the show ground off Ridgeway Road. The next year it was moved to the field at Lark Hill in Thorley Lane where the Red Cross Club stands, and it remained there for the next 20 years. The procession to the field was usually led by the band, with all the Church youth organisations joining in, and the younger children had the treat of riding on a flat lurry pulled by one of Mr. Lewis Garner's shire horses, beautifully decorated with brasses and blue and white flowers.

This followed a tradition of Sunday School treats from the beginning of the century when the older children walked from the Village School and St. Andrew's up to Mr. Austin's field, while the younger ones were taken on a horse lorry lent by Mr. Amos Rogerson of Oak Farm. (Oak Farm stood at the corner of Thorley Lane and Wood Lane, and was later the home of Mr. Shawcross the veterinary surgeon.)

Right: Mr. Garner and his horse in 1960, with a 'load' of assorted 'flowers' with perhaps the odd Brownie as well.

The Housing Boom

Following amalgamation with Altrincham, the 1930s saw a great increase in housing development in Timperley, with the construction of whole new estates. In 1912 work had started on a new road in the Village, later to become Mayfield Road, but by 1934 only two pairs of houses had been completed, and the road had stopped far short of its intended destination – Wood Lane! However plans were then made which included the construction of a housing estate based on new roads connecting with Mayfield Road, which became Vale Road and Perry Road, but were then just part of what was called Manor Park Estate.

Other developments took place in the 1930s off Park Road, the largest being the Riddings estate based on Riddings Road and Sylvan Avenue, but the attractions of Timperley were quoted by various builders for estates all over the area. (See the opposite page.)

Left top: Mayfield Road in the 1920s before the shops in Mayfield Buildings were erected, and with a gravel surface.

Left below: Navigation Station was opened in 1931 when the line was electrified, and the contrast can be seen between the rural scene on the Timperley side of the railway and the housing on the Altrincham side.

The Second World War

During the war the Timperley members of the Auxiliary Fire Service had their headquarters in a builder's sales office at the junction of Stockport Road and the newly constructed Shaftesbury Avenue. They later moved across the road to the stables of 'Thorndale', and then to a large house in Bloomsbury Lane.

Edenhurst, now the Red Cross home on Thorley Lane was the emergency headquarters of the Petroleum Board for the north of England and North Wales in case the HQ at Sunlight House in Quay Street, Manchester was bombed. Two permanent firewatchers were on duty there and were available to help the local team of firewatchers for that part of Thorley Lane, who were led by Mr. Thorp from Thorley Lodge.

Timperley did not suffer a great deal of bomb damage, the area nearest the canal, railways and engineering works in West Timperley getting the worst damage. The air raid of August 1940 caused few problems in Timperley, although the Infants' School on Stockport Road stayed closed for 2 days because of an unexploded bomb in Aimson Place.

The raids during 22nd and 23rd December 1940 caused damage to several houses and a number of casualties: the roads worst hit included Woodhouse Lane East, where 10 houses were damaged, Sylvan Avenue and Westwood Avenue, both of which suffered casualties.

Timperley Auxiliary Fire Service
(L to R):
S. Wilcox, Harold Reed, Bob Unsworth, Theo Schofield and Eddie Pryor. Other members included Ken Bell, Ossie Applewhite, Jack McCardle, Bernard Sweetman and Jack Spurrell.

Left: These houses in Kingsley Road, off Park Road, were some of those to suffer in the blitz of December 1940. This bomb fell on Monday 23rd December, and although several houses were damaged, there were no major casualties.

The Village in the 1950s

Stockport Road in the 1950s. Some changes had taken place since the earlier photos: the big house on the corner, Holly House, had been demolished and the ground made into a car park. Also the signs in the brickwork above the Stonemason's had been altered.

The shops on the left were then occupied by Fred Hill, hairdresser, John Orchard's grocer's shop (he had another shop in Mayfield Buildings). Beyond was Applewhite's butcher's shop and then the Wine Shop and Pryor's greengrocers. On the other side of Thorley Lane, the Co-op stores was added in 1928 and the row of shops in Mayfield Buildings were built in 1930, and although the Village has changed again now, that line of buildings from Thorley Lane to Mayfield Road is still intact.

Broadheath

The Broadheath works of Schaffer and Budenberg, backing onto the Bridgewater Canal, were built in 1914, when the firm moved from its premises in Whitworth Street, Manchester. Being a German owned firm, at the outbreak of the First World War it was nationalised, and then bought back by the Budenberg family after the War. The buildings in the distance are part of the Linotype and Machinery works built in 1896, and the yard on the right belonged to John and Thomas Johnson, timber merchants. This was a well-established firm which in 1871 was employing 15 men and a boy, and even in 1859 was described as "an extensive establishment".

On the other side of the Canal, Atlantic Street was named after the Atlantic Works of George Richards and Co. erected in 1883, which spread to both sides of the street. This view of Atlantic Street about 1914 shows the Lancashire and Yorkshire Bank on the corner, with a branch of the Altrincham Free Library up above. The reading room and lending library were open daily from 7 to 9pm. Beyond this was a block of 8 Cottages called "The Duke's Cottages", which are thought to have been the old Altrincham Workhouse, built in 1756 on a piece of land, "being part of the waste", called Broadheath. The workhouse was used until the mid 19th century, when the new Poor Law Union Workhouse was built at Knutsford. Other firms down Atlantic Street included Thornton-Pickard photographic apparatus makers, then Tilghman's Patent Sand Blast Co. Ltd. and beyond that George Richards Atlantic Works.

Above: Woodfield Road

Opposite page: Atlantic Street

Inset, opposite page: Linotype Munitions Girls
During the First World War, many of the people in Broadheath were involved in war work, including these ladies from the engraving department at Linotype. They include, from the right, back row: Lill Fotherington, Gertie Ratcliffe, Nellie Bradley, and 2 others, middle right: Elsie Hallam, front right: Edie Martin. In 1916, Linotype employed over 1000 people.

PUBLIC LIBRARY AND READING ROOM

LANCASHIRE & YORKSHIRE BANK

BANK

Baguley

Although now part of the City of Manchester, Baguley was for several years included in the Parish of Timperley, until St. John's Church was built on Brooklands Road in 1867. St. John's School was built 12 years later in 1879, on the corner of Wythenshawe Road and Moor Road, and for a time Miss Edith Fitton was schoolmistress there.

Baguley Station was situated between Shady Lane and Brooks's Drive, near to Brooklands Roundabout, and nothing now remains of the station buildings or sidings, except the porter's house on the other side of Brooks Drive. Baguley was the nearest station to Timperley Village, and was the starting point for many outings, especially to the Lancashire Coast resorts. In 1923, the Christ Church Sunday School outing to Southport left Baguley at 8.15am, picked up at West Timperley Station at 8.20 and arrived at Southport at 9.30am. The return fare was 4/3d for adults and for children 2/1½d (21p and 10½p). The station was a popular place for train spotters, as three bridges crossed the track near the station, which had the added interest of the sidings, and a footbridge to the centre platform.

Right top: This view shows the sidings at Baguley Station looking towards Shady Lane bridge. The gentleman with the bowler hat was Mr. George Hankinson, the coal merchant from Orchard Place, Timperley, where he had his coal yard.

Left: Looking towards Timperley, with Brooks's Drive bridge, which was erected in 1870, according to the date on the ironwork of the bridge. This applies to the date that this part of Brooks's road was constructed, after the railway was built. The staff shown here included Mr. Pilling, from Timperley, on the right, Mr. Harry Jackson in the centre, and on the left Mr. John William Wyatt, the Station Master.

Quarry Bank Inn

The Inn gained its name from the quarry which was behind Marston's the builders on the opposite side of Stockport Road. The quarry went out of use in the early 19th century, but was the source of much of the sandstone walling in Timperley, including the walls along Stockport Road. Another quarry lay among the fields which were later cut by Shaftesbury Avenue, and until 1982 this was represented by a small grassed plot between the bungalows. Building has now been allowed on this site thanks to concrete pilings which extend down to the bedrock.

In 1899 the Quarry Bank Inn was run by Thomas Platt, described as a beer retailer and plumber, and the building on the left was occupied by Joseph Clarke, blacksmith.

The pub was re-modelled in 1909 but the smithy remained next door, and beyond that was a coal yard, the merchant being Ernest Jackson.

Things had completely changed by 1916 when James Walker was the landlord, and Harold Platt, plumber, had moved into the smithy, with Aaron Smith taking over the coal depot.

Shaftesbury Avenue

Shaftesbury Avenue was started in the late 1930s, was used for parking military vehicles during the war, and finally opened to traffic, and developed with housing during the 1950s and 1960s which was also the period when the Broomwood Estate was being built.

This view shows the junction with Stockport Road and the parade of shops on the right.